AF280201

ihappy journal

my simple journal

Nalle Windahl

Become happier, reflect, grow and reach your goals.

First edition

Förlag: BoD – Books on Demand, Stockholm, Sverige
Tryck: BoD – Books on Demand, Norderstedt, Tyskland

ISBN: 978-91-7969-215-5

About this book

This is your book, it is about you, your life, your thoughts, dreams and goals.

You decide what to use, everything, some of it or just a little of it. It is a tool that combines many different thoughts and techniques developed by different wise people who have walked these paths before us. Their techniques and tools have helped many others, they have helped me and hopefully, they will help you.

The setup of this book

The first part is a short guide with the basic thoughts behind each part. But it is up to you to choose what parts to use, there are no right or wrong, only what feels right for you!

Other resources

Except the tools and the various parts of this book, you can also find, totally free, a lot of things on www.ihappy.one.

With hopes that you will both enjoy this book and find it use full.

Kind regards,

/Nalle

Your life – your prerequisites – your path

What's the deal?

- Weekly overview
- Seven daily logs
- Weekly summary
- My thoughts after this week
- Then it repeats

What's in the weekly overview?

- Intention of the week
    - How do you want your week to be. Calm? Harmonic? Filled with energy? Something you need to practice or pay extra attention to?
- Focus of the week
    - What would you like to focus on? A certain task or project? A relationship?
- The five most important priorities of the week
    - What five things are most important to you to prioretize this week? A certain task? A meeting? An important birthday? Something that you relly want to prioretize above other important things…
- Three habits you want to track during the week (*This week I will*)
    - Write <u>what</u> you want to d,; i.e "I will go to the gym three times this week." As you have written it, transfer to the daily prioretized tasks in your daily log for the three days. As a reminder to yourself.
    - Explain <u>why</u> you want to do this, i.e. "I want to get more energy and be able to raise my physical capacity." To motivate you when you find it hard to complete what you initially set out to do.
    - Repeat for habit 2 and 3.

What does my daily log contain?

- Date
- Three things you are grateful for
    - o Big or small things. Roof over your head? Your pet? A certain ability you have? People around you? Your favorite cup? A great way to start your day with gratitude journaling!
- Three prioretized tasks
    - o What are your most prioritized tasks for the day? Start your day with reading through or write them down. To keep them fresh in mind.
- A thing that made you happy
    - o In the evening, recall a thing during the day that made you happy.
- Something you learned
    - o In the evening, reflect on something you have learned during the day.
- Your mood
    - o In the evening, choose one or several symbols that reflect you mood during the day. Each symbol means exactly what you want it to mean!
- How have you felt?
    - o In the evening, Good (thumbs up) or bad (thumbs down)?
- Your three habits
    - o How are your three habits progressing? Does everything go according to plan? The habits are the ones you've specified in your weekly overview. They can be the same, week after week, or change as you need and wish. Totally up to you! But today, did you manage to do what you set out to do?

And the weekly summary?

Well, you'll notice, it is a part of the flow of this journal. The thought is that you once a week (perhaps on Sundays) roughly plan your week in the weekly overview, move the five most important tasks to your daily log for the day you intend to do it. Then perhaps use this journal each morning as you prepare for your day, and then again in the end of each day to summarize it. And of course, in before you close your week, do a summary of that as well. This to link each day with the next, and each week with the next. Like a turning wheel, before it can start the next lap it needs to complete the ongoing and get back to its turning starting point.

My thoughts after this week

Take a moment to reflect on the week. Write whatever comes to mind, you have two blank pages. Fill them with what you want!

Enjoy!

^..^

Ah, finally… you are about to start using this book.

But before you do, you need to change mindset and focus, which means that I also need to do that.

Below, you can see a line across the page. Everything below this line, and everything else that follows in this book, is written from your perspective… That is you who is reading this right now. Which means that you (you who are reading) becomes I (I am reading) and me, who is writing this disappears completely. So, you become I, and I disappear, right? Chrystal clear?

Now it is only me who is present here in my book. There is no longer any presence of anybody else, just me, with my own thoughts, my own will on my own path. Right here and right now.

I look forward to use this journal as a tool to help me in my everyday life, to challenge me and help me grow.

I accept the challenge with an open mind and a curiosity to see where this might lead me.

As I prepare to begin, I will give myself patience and use the things I find useful and relevant when I turn the page and find my first Weekly overview.

Weekly overview week:_________ year: 20___

My intention for this week:

My focus for this week:

My top five priorities this week:
1.
2.
3.
4.
5.

This week I will:
1.
Because:

2.
Because:

3.
Because:

Daily log ___ / ___ / ___

Today I am grateful for:

1. ....
2. ....
3. ....

My priorities today:

1. ....
2. ....
3. ....

A thing that made me happy:

....
....
....

This is something I learned today:

....
....
....

Today I felt:

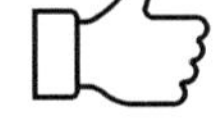

My habits:

1. Yes / No
2. Yes / No
3. Yes / No

My mood today:

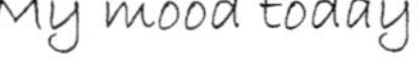

Daily log _____ / _____ / _____

Today I am grateful for:
1. _______________________________
2. _______________________________
3. _______________________________

My priorities today:
1. _______________________________
2. _______________________________
3. _______________________________

A thing that made me happy:
____
____
____

This is something I learned today:
____
____
____

Today I felt:

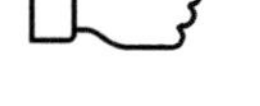

My habits:

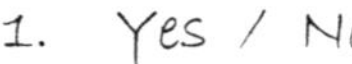
1. Yes / No
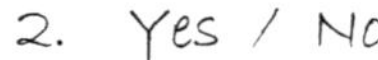
2. Yes / No

3. Yes / No

My mood today:

Daily log _____ / _____ / _____

Today I am grateful for:

1. ________________________________
2. ________________________________
3. ________________________________

My priorities today:

1. ________________________________
2. ________________________________
3. ________________________________

A thing that made me happy:

____

____

____

This is something I learned today:

____

____

____

Today I felt:

My habits:

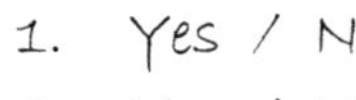

1.   Yes / No
2.   Yes / No
3.   Yes / No

My mood today:

Daily log _____ / _____ / _____

Today I am grateful for:

1. ____
2. ____
3. ____

My priorities today:

1. ____
2. ____
3. ____

A thing that made me happy:

____
____
____

This is something I learned today:

____
____
____

Today I felt:

My habits:

1. Yes / No
2. Yes / No
3. Yes / No

My mood today:

Daily log ____ / ____ / ____

Today I am grateful for:

1. ....
2. ....
3. ....

My priorities today:

1. ....
2. ....
3. ....

A thing that made me happy:

....

....

....

This is something I learned today:

....

....

....

Today I felt:

My habits:

1.   Yes / No
2.   Yes / No
3.   Yes / No

My mood today:

Daily log ____ / ____ / ____

Today I am grateful for:

1. _______________________________________

2. _______________________________________

3. _______________________________________

My priorities today:

1. _______________________________________

2. _______________________________________

3. _______________________________________

A thing that made me happy:

This is something I learned today:

Today I felt:

My habits:

1. Yes / No

2. Yes / No

3. Yes / No

My mood today:

Daily log ___ / ___ / ___

Today I am grateful for:

1.
2.
3.

My priorities today:

1.
2.
3.

A thing that made me happy:

This is something I learned today:

Today I felt:

My habits:

1. Yes / No
2. Yes / No
3. Yes / No

My mood today:

My weekly summary

Which things turned out the way I expected?

____

____

____

What can I do differently another time?

____

____

____

Mostly I felt: 👍 👎

How was my mood this week?

😃 🙂 😐 🙁 😭 😠 😍 😣 🤩 😎 😏 🥴 😮 😈 😇

How well did I keep my habits this week?

☒ ★☆☆ ★★☆ ★★★

My weekly summary - continued

What have I influenced this week?

What did I learn from this?

What have I not been able to influence?

How do I choose to handle it?

o Dwell	o Moping	o Accept
o Let it go	o Ignore	o Joke away
o Learn	o Moody	o Perspective

Other way:

What unfinished tasks do I need to move to next week?

My thoughts after this week

Weekly overview week:________ year: 20__

My intention for this week:

My focus for this week:

My top five priorities this week:
1.
2.
3.
4.
5.

This week I will:
1.
Because:

2.
Because:

3.
Because:

Daily log ___ / ___ / ___

Today I am grateful for:

1. ....

2. ....

3. ....

My priorities today:

1. ....

2. ....

3. ....

A thing that made me happy:

....

....

....

This is something I learned today:

....

....

....

Today I felt:

My habits:

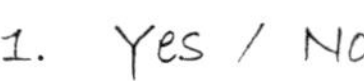
1.   Yes / No

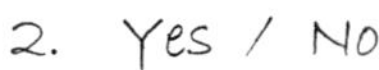
2.   Yes / No

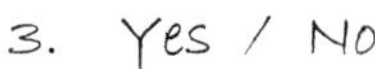
3.   Yes / No

My mood today:

Daily log ____ / ____ / ____

Today I am grateful for:

1. _______________________________________
2. _______________________________________
3. _______________________________________

My priorities today:

1. _______________________________________
2. _______________________________________
3. _______________________________________

A thing that made me happy:

____
____
____

This is something I learned today:

____
____
____

Today I felt:

My habits:

1. Yes / No
2. Yes / No
3. Yes / No

My mood today:

Daily log ____ / ____ / ____

Today I am grateful for:
1.
2.
3.

My priorities today:
1.
2.
3.

A thing that made me happy:

This is something I learned today:

Today I felt:

My habits:

1. Yes / No
2. Yes / No
3. Yes / No

My mood today:

Daily log ___ / ___ / ___

Today I am grateful for:

1. ___________________________
2. ___________________________
3. ___________________________

My priorities today:

1. ___________________________
2. ___________________________
3. ___________________________

A thing that made me happy:

____
____
____

This is something I learned today:

____
____
____

Today I felt:

My habits:

1. Yes / No
2. Yes / No
3. Yes / No

My mood today:

Daily log ______ / ______ / ______

Today I am grateful for:

1. ....
2. ....
3. ....

My priorities today:

1. ....
2. ....
3. ....

A thing that made me happy:

....

....

....

This is something I learned today:

....

....

....

Today I felt:

My habits:

1.   Yes / No
2.   Yes / No
3.   Yes / No

My mood today:

Daily log ___ / ___ / ___

Today I am grateful for:

1. _______________________________________

2. _______________________________________

3. _______________________________________

My priorities today:

1. _______________________________________

2. _______________________________________

3. _______________________________________

A thing that made me happy:

____

____

____

This is something I learned today:

____

____

____

Today I felt:

My habits:

1. Yes / No
2. Yes / No
3. Yes / No

My mood today:

Daily log ___ / ___ / ___

Today I am grateful for:

1. ....
2. ....
3. ....

My priorities today:

1. ....
2. ....
3. ....

A thing that made me happy:

This is something I learned today:

Today I felt:

My habits:

1. Yes / No
2. Yes / No
3. Yes / No

My mood today:

My weekly summary

Which things turned out the way I expected?

What can I do differently another time?

Mostly I felt:

How was my mood this week?

How well did I keep my habits this week?

My weekly summary - continued

What have I influenced this week?

What did I learn from this?

What have I not been able to influence?

How do I choose to handle it?

- o Dwell
- o Let it go
- o Learn

- o Moping
- o Ignore
- o Moody

- o Accept
- o Joke away
- o Perspective

Other way:

What unfinished tasks do I need to move to next week?

My thoughts after this week

Weekly overview week:__________ year: 20__

My intention for this week:

My focus for this week:

My top five priorities this week:
1.
2.
3.
4.
5.

This week I will:
1.
Because:

2.
Because:

3.
Because:

Daily log ____ / ____ / ____

Today I am grateful for:

1. ______________________________
2. ______________________________
3. ______________________________

My priorities today:

1. ______________________________
2. ______________________________
3. ______________________________

A thing that made me happy:

____
____
____

This is something I learned today:

____
____
____

Today I felt:

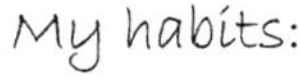

My habits:

1. Yes / No
2. Yes / No
3. Yes / No

My mood today:

Daily log ___ / ___ / ___

Today I am grateful for:

1. ____
2. ____
3. ____

My priorities today:

1. ____
2. ____
3. ____

A thing that made me happy:

____
____
____

This is something I learned today:

____
____
____

Today I felt:

My habits:

1. Yes / No
2. Yes / No
3. Yes / No

My mood today:

Daily log ___ / ___ / ___

Today I am grateful for:

1. ....
2. ....
3. ....

My priorities today:

1. ....
2. ....
3. ....

A thing that made me happy:

....

....

....

This is something I learned today:

....

....

....

Today I felt:

My habits:

1.   Yes / No
2.   Yes / No
3.   Yes / No

My mood today:

Daily log ___ / ___ / ___

Today I am grateful for:
1. _______________________________________
2. _______________________________________
3. _______________________________________

My priorities today:
1. _______________________________________
2. _______________________________________
3. _______________________________________

A thing that made me happy:
____
____
____

This is something I learned today:
____
____
____

Today I felt:

My habits:

1. Yes / No
2. Yes / No
3. Yes / No

My mood today:

Daily log   ___ / ___ / ___

Today I am grateful for:

1. ________________________________
2. ________________________________
3. ________________________________

My priorities today:

1. ________________________________
2. ________________________________
3. ________________________________

A thing that made me happy:

____
____
____

This is something I learned today:

____
____
____

Today I felt:

My habits:

1. Yes / No
2. Yes / No
3. Yes / No

My mood today:

Daily log   /   /

Today I am grateful for:
1.
2.
3.

My priorities today:
1.
2.
3.

A thing that made me happy:

This is something I learned today:

Today I felt:

My habits:

1. Yes / No
2. Yes / No
3. Yes / No

My mood today:

Daily log ___ / ___ / ___

Today I am grateful for:

1. ___
2. ___
3. ___

My priorities today:

1. ___
2. ___
3. ___

A thing that made me happy:

This is something I learned today:

Today I felt:

My habits:

1. Yes / No
2. Yes / No
3. Yes / No

My mood today:

My weekly summary

Which things turned out the way I expected?

What can I do differently another time?

Mostly I felt: 👍 👎

How was my mood this week?

How well did I keep my habits this week?

My weekly summary - continued

What have I influenced this week?

What did I learn from this?

What have I not been able to influence?

How do I choose to handle it?

- o Dwell
- o Let it go
- o Learn
- o Moping
- o Ignore
- o Moody
- o Accept
- o Joke away
- o Perspective

Other way:

What unfinished tasks do I need to move to next week?

My thoughts after this week

Weekly overview week:_____________ year: 20___

My intention for this week:

My focus for this week:

My top five priorities this week:
1.
2.
3.
4.
5.

This week I will:
1.
Because:

2.
Because:

3.
Because:

Daily log   ___ / ___ / ___

Today I am grateful for:

1. ____
2. ____
3. ____

My priorities today:

1. ____
2. ____
3. ____

A thing that made me happy:

____
____
____

This is something I learned today:

____
____
____

Today I felt:

My habits:

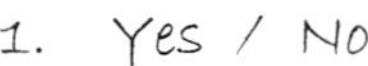
1. Yes / No
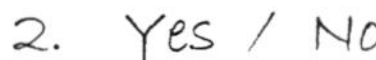
2. Yes / No
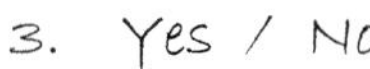
3. Yes / No

My mood today:

Daily log ____ / ____ / ____

Today I am grateful for:

1.
2.
3.

My priorities today:

1.
2.
3.

A thing that made me happy:

This is something I learned today:

Today I felt:

My habits:

1. Yes / No
2. Yes / No
3. Yes / No

My mood today:

Daily log ____ / ____ / ____

Today I am grateful for:
1. ____
2. ____
3. ____

My priorities today:
1. ____
2. ____
3. ____

A thing that made me happy:
____
____
____

This is something I learned today:
____
____
____

Today I felt:

My habits:

1. Yes / No
2. Yes / No
3. Yes / No

My mood today:

Daily log _____ / _____ / _____

Today I am grateful for:

1. _______________________________
2. _______________________________
3. _______________________________

My priorities today:

1. _______________________________
2. _______________________________
3. _______________________________

A thing that made me happy:

____
____
____

This is something I learned today:

____
____
____

Today I felt:

My habits:

1. Yes / No
2. Yes / No
3. Yes / No

My mood today:

Daily log ____ / ____ / ____

Today I am grateful for:

1.
2.
3.

My priorities today:

1.
2.
3.

A thing that made me happy:

This is something I learned today:

Today I felt:

My habits:

1. Yes / No
2. Yes / No
3. Yes / No

My mood today:

Daily log ___ / ___ / ___

Today I am grateful for:
1. _______________________________
2. _______________________________
3. _______________________________

My priorities today:
1. _______________________________
2. _______________________________
3. _______________________________

A thing that made me happy:
____
____
____

This is something I learned today:
____
____
____

Today I felt:

My habits:

1. Yes / No
2. Yes / No
3. Yes / No

My mood today:

Daily log ___ / ___ / ___

Today I am grateful for:

1. ....

2. ....

3. ....

My priorities today:

1. ....

2. ....

3. ....

A thing that made me happy:

....

....

....

This is something I learned today:

....

....

....

Today I felt:

My habits:

1. Yes / No
2. Yes / No
3. Yes / No

My mood today:

My weekly summary

Which things turned out the way I expected?

What can I do differently another time?

Mostly I felt: 👍 👎

How was my mood this week?

😀 🙂 😌 🙁 😭 😟 😍 😖 🤩 😎 😐 🥴 😮 😈 😊

How well did I keep my habits this week?

☒ ⭐☆☆ ⭐⭐☆ ⭐⭐⭐

What have I influenced this week?

What did I learn from this?

What have I not been able to influence?

How do I choose to handle it?

- o   Dwell
- o   Let it go
- o   Learn

- o   Moping
- o   Ignore
- o   Moody

- o   Accept
- o   Joke away
- o   Perspective

Other way:

What unfinished tasks do I need to move to next week?

My thoughts after this week

Weekly overview week:_____________ year: 20___

My intention for this week:

My focus for this week:

My top five priorities this week:
1.
2.
3.
4.
5.

This week I will:
1.
Because:

2.
Because:

3.
Because:

Daily log   /   /

Today I am grateful for:
1.
2.
3.

My priorities today:
1.
2.
3.

A thing that made me happy:

This is something I learned today:

Today I felt: My habits:

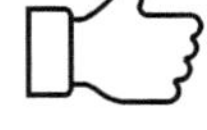      1.   Yes / No
                                           2.   Yes / No
                                           3.   Yes / No

My mood today:

Daily log   /   /

Today I am grateful for:
1.
2.
3.

My priorities today:
1.
2.
3.

A thing that made me happy:

This is something I learned today:

Today I felt:

My habits:

1.   Yes / No
2.   Yes / No
3.   Yes / No

My mood today:

Daily log ____ / ____ / ____

Today I am grateful for:

1.
2.
3.

My priorities today:

1.
2.
3.

A thing that made me happy:

This is something I learned today:

Today I felt:

My habits:

1. Yes / No
2. Yes / No
3. Yes / No

My mood today:

Daily log _____ / _____ / _____

Today I am grateful for:

1. _______________________________________
2. _______________________________________
3. _______________________________________

My priorities today:

1. _______________________________________
2. _______________________________________
3. _______________________________________

A thing that made me happy:

____
____
____

This is something I learned today:

____
____
____

Today I felt:

My habits:

1. Yes / No
2. Yes / No
3. Yes / No

My mood today:

Daily log _____ / _____ / _____

Today I am grateful for:
1. ____
2. ____
3. ____

My priorities today:
1. ____
2. ____
3. ____

A thing that made me happy:

____
____
____

This is something I learned today:

____
____
____

Today I felt:

My habits:

1. Yes / No
2. Yes / No
3. Yes / No

My mood today:

Daily log ___/___/___

Today I am grateful for:

1. ______________________________
2. ______________________________
3. ______________________________

My priorities today:

1. ______________________________
2. ______________________________
3. ______________________________

A thing that made me happy:

____
____
____

This is something I learned today:

____
____

Today I felt:

My habits:

1. Yes / No
2. Yes / No
3. Yes / No

My mood today:

Daily log   ___ / ___ / ___

Today I am grateful for:

1.
2.
3.

My priorities today:

1.
2.
3.

A thing that made me happy:

This is something I learned today:

Today I felt:

My habits:

1.   Yes / No
2.   Yes / No
3.   Yes / No

My mood today:

My weekly summary

Which things turned out the way I expected?

What can I do differently another time?

Mostly I felt:

How was my mood this week?

How well did I keep my habits this week?

My weekly summary - continued

What have I influenced this week?

What did I learn from this?

What have I not been able to influence?

How do I choose to handle it?

o Dwell	o Moping	o Accept
o Let it go	o Ignore	o Joke away
o Learn	o Moody	o Perspective

Other way:

What unfinished tasks do I need to move to next week?

My thoughts after this week

Weekly overview week:__________ year: 20__

My intention for this week:

My focus for this week:

My top five priorities this week:
1.
2.
3.
4.
5.

This week I will:
1.
Because:

2.
Because:

3.
Because:

Daily log ___ / ___ / ___

Today I am grateful for:

1. ______________________
2. ______________________
3. ______________________

My priorities today:

1. ______________________
2. ______________________
3. ______________________

A thing that made me happy:

____
____
____

This is something I learned today:

____
____
____

Today I felt:

My habits:

1. Yes / No
2. Yes / No
3. Yes / No

My mood today:

Daily log _____ / _____ / _____

Today I am grateful for:
1.
2.
3.

My priorities today:
1.
2.
3.

A thing that made me happy:

This is something I learned today:

Today I felt:

My habits:

1.   Yes / No
2.   Yes / No
3.   Yes / No

My mood today:

Daily log ____ / ____ / ____

Today I am grateful for:

1. ______________________________
2. ______________________________
3. ______________________________

My priorities today:

1. ______________________________
2. ______________________________
3. ______________________________

A thing that made me happy:

____
____
____

This is something I learned today:

____
____
____

Today I felt:

My habits:

1.   Yes / No
2.   Yes / No
3.   Yes / No

My mood today:

Daily log ___ / ___ / ___

Today I am grateful for:

1. _______________________________

2. _______________________________

3. _______________________________

My priorities today:

1. _______________________________

2. _______________________________

3. _______________________________

A thing that made me happy:

____

____

____

This is something I learned today:

____

____

____

Today I felt:

My habits:

1. Yes / No
2. Yes / No
3. Yes / No

My mood today:

Daily log ____ / ____ / ____

Today I am grateful for:
1. _______________________________________
2. _______________________________________
3. _______________________________________

My priorities today:
1. _______________________________________
2. _______________________________________
3. _______________________________________

A thing that made me happy:
____
____
____

This is something I learned today:
____
____
____

Today I felt:

My habits:

1. Yes / No
2. Yes / No
3. Yes / No

My mood today:

Daily log ____ / ____ / ____

Today I am grateful for:
1. _______________________
2. _______________________
3. _______________________

My priorities today:
1. _______________________
2. _______________________
3. _______________________

A thing that made me happy:
____
____
____

This is something I learned today:
____
____
____

Today I felt:

My habits:

1. Yes / No
2. Yes / No
3. Yes / No

My mood today:

Daily log ___ / ___ / ___

Today I am grateful for:
1.
2.
3.

My priorities today:
1.
2.
3.

A thing that made me happy:

This is something I learned today:

Today I felt:

My habits:

1. Yes / No
2. Yes / No
3. Yes / No

My mood today:

My weekly summary

Which things turned out the way I expected?

____

____

____

What can I do differently another time?

____

____

____

Mostly I felt: 👍 👎

How was my mood this week?

😀 🙂 😐 🙁 😭 😧 😍 😖 🤩 😎 😉 🥴 😮 😈 😇

How well did I keep my habits this week?

☒   ★☆☆   ★★☆   ★★★

My weekly summary - continued

What have I influenced this week?

What did I learn from this?

What have I not been able to influence?

How do I choose to handle it?

o Dwell	o Moping	o Accept
o Let it go	o Ignore	o Joke away
o Learn	o Moody	o Perspective

Other way:

What unfinished tasks do I need to move to next week?

Weekly overview week:_____________ year: 20___

My intention for this week:

My focus for this week:

My top five priorities this week:
1.
2.
3.
4.
5.

This week I will:
1.
Because:

2.
Because:

3.
Because:

Daily log   /   /

Today I am grateful for:
1.
2.
3.

My priorities today:
1.
2.
3.

A thing that made me happy:

This is something I learned today:

Today I felt:

My habits:

1.   Yes / No
2.   Yes / No
3.   Yes / No

My mood today:

Daily log ____/____/____

Today I am grateful for:

1. ____

2. ____

3. ____

My priorities today:

1. ____

2. ____

3. ____

A thing that made me happy:

____

____

This is something I learned today:

____

____

Today I felt:

My habits:

1. Yes / No

2. Yes / No

3. Yes / No

My mood today:

Daily log ____ / ____ / ____

Today I am grateful for:

1. ______________________________
2. ______________________________
3. ______________________________

My priorities today:

1. ______________________________
2. ______________________________
3. ______________________________

A thing that made me happy:

____
____
____

This is something I learned today:

____
____

Today I felt:

My habits:

1. Yes / No
2. Yes / No
3. Yes / No

My mood today:

Daily log ___ / ___ / ___

Today I am grateful for:

1.
2.
3.

My priorities today:

1.
2.
3.

A thing that made me happy:

This is something I learned today:

Today I felt:

My habits:

1. Yes / No
2. Yes / No
3. Yes / No

My mood today:

Daily log   /   /

Today I am grateful for:
1.
2.
3.

My priorities today:
1.
2.
3.

A thing that made me happy:

This is something I learned today:

Today I felt:

My habits:

1.   Yes / No
2.   Yes / No
3.   Yes / No

My mood today:

Daily log ___/___/___

Today I am grateful for:

1. _______________________________
2. _______________________________
3. _______________________________

My priorities today:

1. _______________________________
2. _______________________________
3. _______________________________

A thing that made me happy:

____

____

____

This is something I learned today:

____

____

____

Today I felt: My habits:

1. Yes / No
2. Yes / No
3. Yes / No

My mood today:

Daily log _____ / _____ / _____

Today I am grateful for:

1. ....
2. ....
3. ....

My priorities today:

1. ....
2. ....
3. ....

A thing that made me happy:

....

....

....

This is something I learned today:

....

....

....

Today I felt:

My habits:

1.   Yes / No
2.   Yes / No
3.   Yes / No

My mood today:

My weekly summary

Which things turned out the way I expected?

What can I do differently another time?

Mostly I felt:

How was my mood this week?

How well did I keep my habits this week?

My weekly summary - continued

What have I influenced this week?

What did I learn from this?

What have I not been able to influence?

How do I choose to handle it?

o Dwell	o Moping	o Accept
o Let it go	o Ignore	o Joke away
o Learn	o Moody	o Perspective

Other way:

What unfinished tasks do I need to move to next week?

Weekly overview week:__________ year: 20__

My intention for this week:

My focus for this week:

My top five priorities this week:
1.
2.
3.
4.
5.

This week I will:
1.
Because:

2.
Because:

3.
Because:

Daily log ____ / ____ / ____

Today I am grateful for:
1. ______________________________
2. ______________________________
3. ______________________________

My priorities today:
1. ______________________________
2. ______________________________
3. ______________________________

A thing that made me happy:
____
____
____

This is something I learned today:
____
____
____

Today I felt:

My habits:

1. Yes / No
2. Yes / No
3. Yes / No

My mood today:

Daily log _____ / _____ / _____

Today I am grateful for:
1. ____
2. ____
3. ____

My priorities today:
1. ____
2. ____
3. ____

A thing that made me happy:

This is something I learned today:

Today I felt:

My habits:

1. Yes / No
2. Yes / No
3. Yes / No

My mood today:

Daily log _____ / _____ / _____

Today I am grateful for:

1. ____
2. ____
3. ____

My priorities today:

1. ____
2. ____
3. ____

A thing that made me happy:

____

____

____

This is something I learned today:

____

____

____

Today I felt:

My habits:

1. Yes / No
2. Yes / No
3. Yes / No

My mood today:

Daily log ___ / ___ / ___

Today I am grateful for:

1. _______________________________________

2. _______________________________________

3. _______________________________________

My priorities today:

1. _______________________________________

2. _______________________________________

3. _______________________________________

A thing that made me happy:

____

____

This is something I learned today:

____

____

Today I felt:

My habits:

1.   Yes / No

2.   Yes / No

3.   Yes / No

My mood today:

Daily log   /   /

Today I am grateful for:
1.
2.
3.

My priorities today:
1.
2.
3.

A thing that made me happy:

This is something I learned today:

Today I felt:

My habits:

1. Yes / No
2. Yes / No
3. Yes / No

My mood today:

Daily log ___ / ___ / ___

Today I am grateful for:
1. ___________________________________
2. ___________________________________
3. ___________________________________

My priorities today:
1. ___________________________________
2. ___________________________________
3. ___________________________________

A thing that made me happy:
____
____
____

This is something I learned today:
____
____
____

Today I felt:

My habits:

1. Yes / No
2. Yes / No
3. Yes / No

My mood today:

Daily log ____ / ____ / ____

Today I am grateful for:
1.
2.
3.

My priorities today:
1.
2.
3.

A thing that made me happy:

This is something I learned today:

Today I felt:

My habits:

1. Yes / No
2. Yes / No
3. Yes / No

My mood today:

My weekly summary

Which things turned out the way I expected?

What can I do differently another time?

Mostly I felt: 👍 👎

How was my mood this week?

😀 😊 😐 ☹️ 😭 😟 😍 😖 🤩 😎 😉 😳 😮 😈 😊

How well did I keep my habits this week?

☒ ★☆☆ ★★☆ ★★★

My weekly summary - continued

What have I influenced this week?

What did I learn from this?

What have I not been able to influence?

How do I choose to handle it?

- o Dwell
- o Let it go
- o Learn
- o Moping
- o Ignore
- o Moody
- o Accept
- o Joke away
- o Perspective

Other way:

What unfinished tasks do I need to move to next week?

Weekly overview week:__________ year: 20__

My intention for this week:

My focus for this week:

My top five priorities this week:
1.
2.
3.
4.
5.

This week I will:
1.
Because:

2.
Because:

3.
Because:

Daily log ___ / ___ / ___

Today I am grateful for:

1. ______________________________
2. ______________________________
3. ______________________________

My priorities today:

1. ______________________________
2. ______________________________
3. ______________________________

A thing that made me happy:

____
____
____

This is something I learned today:

____
____
____

Today I felt:

My habits:

1. Yes / No
2. Yes / No
3. Yes / No

My mood today:

Daily log ___ / ___ / ___

Today I am grateful for:

1. ____
2. ____
3. ____

My priorities today:

1. ____
2. ____
3. ____

A thing that made me happy:

____

____

____

This is something I learned today:

____

____

____

Today I felt:

My habits:

1. Yes / No
2. Yes / No
3. Yes / No

My mood today:

Daily log ___ / ___ / ___

Today I am grateful for:

1. ____

2. ____

3. ____

My priorities today:

1. ____

2. ____

3. ____

A thing that made me happy:

____

____

____

This is something I learned today:

____

____

____

Today I felt: My habits:

    1.   Yes / No
    2.   Yes / No
    3.   Yes / No

My mood today:

Daily log _____ / _____ / _____

Today I am grateful for:
1. _______________________________
2. _______________________________
3. _______________________________

My priorities today:
1. _______________________________
2. _______________________________
3. _______________________________

A thing that made me happy:
____
____
____

This is something I learned today:
____
____
____

Today I felt:

My habits:

1. Yes / No
2. Yes / No
3. Yes / No

My mood today:

Daily log _____ / _____ / _____

Today I am grateful for:

1. ....
2. ....
3. ....

My priorities today:

1. ....
2. ....
3. ....

A thing that made me happy:

....

....

....

This is something I learned today:

....

....

Today I felt:

My habits:

1. Yes / No
2. Yes / No
3. Yes / No

My mood today:

Daily log _____ / _____ / _____

Today I am grateful for:

1. _______________________________________

2. _______________________________________

3. _______________________________________

My priorities today:

1. _______________________________________

2. _______________________________________

3. _______________________________________

A thing that made me happy:

____

____

____

This is something I learned today:

____

____

____

Today I felt:

My habits:

1. Yes / No

2. Yes / No

3. Yes / No

My mood today:

Daily log   ___ / ___ / ___

Today I am grateful for:

1. ....
2. ....
3. ....

My priorities today:

1. ....
2. ....
3. ....

A thing that made me happy:

....

....

....

This is something I learned today:

....

....

....

Today I felt:

My habits:

1.   Yes / No
2.   Yes / No
3.   Yes / No

My mood today:

My weekly summary

Which things turned out the way I expected?

What can I do differently another time?

Mostly I felt:

How was my mood this week?

How well did I keep my habits this week?

My weekly summary - continued

What have I influenced this week?

What did I learn from this?

What have I not been able to influence?

How do I choose to handle it?

o Dwell	o Moping	o Accept
o Let it go	o Ignore	o Joke away
o Learn	o Moody	o Perspective

Other way:

What unfinished tasks do I need to move to next week?

My thoughts after this week

Weekly overview week:__________ year: 20__

My intention for this week:

My focus for this week:

My top five priorities this week:
1.
2.
3.
4.
5.

This week I will:
1.
Because:

2.
Because:

3.
Because:

Daily log ____ / ____ / ____

Today I am grateful for:

1. _______________________________

2. _______________________________

3. _______________________________

My priorities today:

1. _______________________________

2. _______________________________

3. _______________________________

A thing that made me happy:

____

____

____

This is something I learned today:

____

____

____

Today I felt:

My habits:

1. Yes / No
2. Yes / No
3. Yes / No

My mood today:

Daily log ____ / ____ / ____

Today I am grateful for:
1. _______________
2. _______________
3. _______________

My priorities today:
1. _______________
2. _______________
3. _______________

A thing that made me happy:

____
____
____

This is something I learned today:

____
____
____

Today I felt:

My habits:

1. Yes / No
2. Yes / No
3. Yes / No

My mood today:

Daily log ___ / ___ / ___

Today I am grateful for:

1. ________________________________
2. ________________________________
3. ________________________________

My priorities today:

1. ________________________________
2. ________________________________
3. ________________________________

A thing that made me happy:

____

____

____

This is something I learned today:

____

____

____

Today I felt:

My habits:

1. Yes / No
2. Yes / No
3. Yes / No

My mood today:

Daily log   /   /

Today I am grateful for:
1.
2.
3.

My priorities today:
1.
2.
3.

A thing that made me happy:

This is something I learned today:

Today I felt:

My habits:

1.   Yes / No
2.   Yes / No
3.   Yes / No

My mood today:

Daily log ____ / ____ / ____

Today I am grateful for:
1.
2.
3.

My priorities today:
1.
2.
3.

A thing that made me happy:

This is something I learned today:

Today I felt:

My habits:

1. Yes / No
2. Yes / No
3. Yes / No

My mood today:

           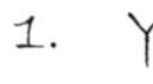   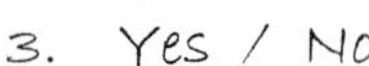

Today I am grateful for:
1. _______________________________
2. _______________________________
3. _______________________________

My priorities today:
1. _______________________________
2. _______________________________
3. _______________________________

A thing that made me happy:
____
____
____

This is something I learned today:
____
____

Today I felt:

My habits:

1.   Yes / No
2.   Yes / No
3.   Yes / No

My mood today:

Daily log ____ / ____ / ____

Today I am grateful for:

1. ________________________________
2. ________________________________
3. ________________________________

My priorities today:

1. ________________________________
2. ________________________________
3. ________________________________

A thing that made me happy:

____

____

____

This is something I learned today:

____

____

____

Today I felt:

My habits:

1. Yes / No
2. Yes / No
3. Yes / No

My mood today:

My weekly summary

Which things turned out the way I expected?

What can I do differently another time?

Mostly I felt:

How was my mood this week?

How well did I keep my habits this week?

My weekly summary - continued

What have I influenced this week?

What did I learn from this?

What have I not been able to influence?

How do I choose to handle it?

o Dwell	o Moping	o Accept
o Let it go	o Ignore	o Joke away
o Learn	o Moody	o Perspective

Other way:

What unfinished tasks do I need to move to next week?

Weekly overview week:_____________ year: 20___

My intention for this week:

My focus for this week:

My top five priorities this week:
1.
2.
3.
4.
5.

This week I will:
1.
Because:

2.
Because:

3.
Because:

Daily log ___ / ___ / ___

Today I am grateful for:

1. ....

2. ....

3. ....

My priorities today:

1. ....

2. ....

3. ....

A thing that made me happy:

....

....

....

This is something I learned today:

....

....

....

Today I felt:

My habits:

1. Yes / No

2. Yes / No

3. Yes / No

My mood today:

Daily log ___ / ___ / ___

Today I am grateful for:
1.
2.
3.

My priorities today:
1.
2.
3.

A thing that made me happy:

This is something I learned today:

Today I felt:

My habits:

1.   Yes / No
2.   Yes / No
3.   Yes / No

My mood today:

Daily log _____ / _____ / _____

Today I am grateful for:

1. ....
2. ....
3. ....

My priorities today:

1. ....
2. ....
3. ....

A thing that made me happy:

....

....

....

This is something I learned today:

....

....

....

Today I felt:

My habits:

1.　Yes / No
2.　Yes / No
3.　Yes / No

My mood today:

😃 🙂 😐 🙁 😭 😦 😍 😖 🤩 😎 😌 🤢 😲 😈 😇

Daily log   /   /

Today I am grateful for:
1.
2.
3.

My priorities today:
1.
2.
3.

A thing that made me happy:

This is something I learned today:

Today I felt:

My habits:

1. Yes / No
2. Yes / No
3. Yes / No

My mood today:

Daily log ___ / ___ / ___

Today I am grateful for:
1.
2.
3.

My priorities today:
1.
2.
3.

A thing that made me happy:

This is something I learned today:

Today I felt:

My habits:

1. Yes / No
2. Yes / No
3. Yes / No

My mood today:

Daily log ___/___/___

Today I am grateful for:

1. _______________________________
2. _______________________________
3. _______________________________

My priorities today:

1. _______________________________
2. _______________________________
3. _______________________________

A thing that made me happy:

____
____
____

This is something I learned today:

____
____

Today I felt:

My habits:

1. Yes / No
2. Yes / No
3. Yes / No

My mood today:

Daily log ___ / ___ / ___

Today I am grateful for:

1. ....
2. ....
3. ....

My priorities today:

1. ....
2. ....
3. ....

A thing that made me happy:

....

....

....

This is something I learned today:

....

....

....

Today I felt:

My habits:

1. Yes / No
2. Yes / No
3. Yes / No

My mood today:

My weekly summary

Which things turned out the way I expected?

What can I do differently another time?

Mostly I felt:

How was my mood this week?

How well did I keep my habits this week?

My weekly summary - continued

What have I influenced this week?

What did I learn from this?

What have I not been able to influence?

How do I choose to handle it?

o Dwell	o Moping	o Accept
o Let it go	o Ignore	o Joke away
o Learn	o Moody	o Perspective

Other way:

What unfinished tasks do I need to move to next week?

My thoughts after this week

Weekly overview week:_____________ year: 20___

My intention for this week:

My focus for this week:

My top five priorities this week:
1.
2.
3.
4.
5.

This week I will:
1.
Because:

2.
Because:

3.
Because:

Daily log ____ / ____ / ________

Today I am grateful for:

1. ....
2. ....
3. ....

My priorities today:

1. ....
2. ....
3. ....

A thing that made me happy:

This is something I learned today:

Today I felt:

My habits:

1. Yes / No
2. Yes / No
3. Yes / No

My mood today:

Daily log ___ / ___ / ___

Today I am grateful for:
1. _______________________________
2. _______________________________
3. _______________________________

My priorities today:
1. _______________________________
2. _______________________________
3. _______________________________

A thing that made me happy:
____
____
____

This is something I learned today:
____
____
____

Today I felt:

My habits:

1. Yes / No
2. Yes / No
3. Yes / No

My mood today:

Daily log ___ / ___ /___

Today I am grateful for:

1.
2.
3.

My priorities today:

1.
2.
3.

A thing that made me happy:

This is something I learned today:

Today I felt:

My habits:

1. Yes / No
2. Yes / No
3. Yes / No

My mood today:

Daily log   /   /

Today I am grateful for:
1.
2.
3.

My priorities today:
1.
2.
3.

A thing that made me happy:

This is something I learned today:

Today I felt:

My habits:

1.   Yes / No
2.   Yes / No
3.   Yes / No

My mood today:

Daily log ____ / ____ / ____

Today I am grateful for:

1.
2.
3.

My priorities today:

1.
2.
3.

A thing that made me happy:

This is something I learned today:

Today I felt:

My habits:

1. Yes / No
2. Yes / No
3. Yes / No

My mood today:

Daily log   /   /

Today I am grateful for:
1.
2.
3.

My priorities today:
1.
2.
3.

A thing that made me happy:

This is something I learned today:

Today I felt:

My habits:

1.   Yes / No
2.   Yes / No
3.   Yes / No

My mood today:

Daily log ___ / ___ / ___

Today I am grateful for:

1. ....
2. ....
3. ....

My priorities today:

1. ....
2. ....
3. ....

A thing that made me happy:

....

....

....

This is something I learned today:

....

....

....

Today I felt: My habits:

                                                  1.   Yes / No
                                                  2.   Yes / No
                                                  3.   Yes / No

My mood today:

My weekly summary

Which things turned out the way I expected?

What can I do differently another time?

Mostly I felt: 👍 👎

How was my mood this week?

😃 😊 😐 😟 😭 😦 😍 😖 🤩 😎 😌 😋 😮 😈 😇

How well did I keep my habits this week?

☒ ★☆☆ ★★☆ ★★★

My weekly summary - continued

What have I influenced this week?

What did I learn from this?

What have I not been able to influence?

How do I choose to handle it?

o Dwell	o Moping	o Accept
o Let it go	o Ignore	o Joke away
o Learn	o Moody	o Perspective

Other way:

What unfinished tasks do I need to move to next week?

Weekly overview week:__________ year: 20__

My intention for this week:

My focus for this week:

My top five priorities this week:
1.
2.
3.
4.
5.

This week I will:
1.
Because:

2.
Because:

3.
Because:

Daily log ____ / ____ / ____

Today I am grateful for:

1.

2.

3.

My priorities today:

1.

2.

3.

A thing that made me happy:

This is something I learned today:

Today I felt: My habits:

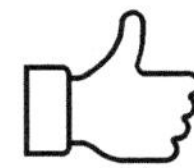 

    1.   Yes / No

    2.   Yes / No

    3.   Yes / No

My mood today:

Daily log ___ / ___ / ___

Today I am grateful for:

1. ___________________________
2. ___________________________
3. ___________________________

My priorities today:

1. ___________________________
2. ___________________________
3. ___________________________

A thing that made me happy:

____
____
____

This is something I learned today:

____
____
____

Today I felt:

My habits:

1. Yes / No
2. Yes / No
3. Yes / No

My mood today:

Daily log _____ / _____ /

Today I am grateful for:
1.
2.
3.

My priorities today:
1.
2.
3.

A thing that made me happy:

This is something I learned today:

Today I felt:

My habits:

1. Yes / No
2. Yes / No
3. Yes / No

My mood today:

Daily log ___ / ___ / ___

Today I am grateful for:
1. _______________________________
2. _______________________________
3. _______________________________

My priorities today:
1. _______________________________
2. _______________________________
3. _______________________________

A thing that made me happy:
____
____
____

This is something I learned today:
____
____
____

Today I felt:

My habits:

1. Yes / No
2. Yes / No
3. Yes / No

My mood today:

Daily log ___ / ___ / ___

Today I am grateful for:

1.

2.

3.

My priorities today:

1.

2.

3.

A thing that made me happy:

This is something I learned today:

Today I felt:

My habits:

1. Yes / No
2. Yes / No
3. Yes / No

My mood today:

😃 🙂 😐 🙁 😭 😟 😍 😖 🤩 😎 😌 😵 😲 😈 😇

Daily log _____ / _____ / _____

Today I am grateful for:

1. ....
2. ....
3. ....

My priorities today:

1. ....
2. ....
3. ....

A thing that made me happy:

....

....

....

This is something I learned today:

....

....

Today I felt:

My habits:

1. Yes / No
2. Yes / No
3. Yes / No

My mood today:

Daily log ____ / ____ /

Today I am grateful for:

1.
2.
3.

My priorities today:

1.
2.
3.

A thing that made me happy:

This is something I learned today:

Today I felt:

My habits:

1.   Yes / No
2.   Yes / No
3.   Yes / No

My mood today:

My weekly summary

Which things turned out the way I expected?

What can I do differently another time?

Mostly I felt: 👍 👎

How was my mood this week?

😀 😊 😐 ☹️ 😭 😠 😍 😖 🤩 😎 😌 🥴 😮 😈 😇

How well did I keep my habits this week?

☒   ★☆☆   ★★☆   ★★★

My weekly summary - continued

What have I influenced this week?

What did I learn from this?

What have I not been able to influence?

How do I choose to handle it?

o Dwell	o Moping	o Accept
o Let it go	o Ignore	o Joke away
o Learn	o Moody	o Perspective

Other way:

What unfinished tasks do I need to move to next week?

My thoughts after this week

My intention for this week:

My focus for this week:

My top five priorities this week:
1.
2.
3.
4.
5.

This week I will:
1.
Because:

2.
Because:

3.
Because:

Daily log ___ / ___ / ___

Today I am grateful for:

1. ____
2. ____
3. ____

My priorities today:

1. ____
2. ____
3. ____

A thing that made me happy:

____
____
____

This is something I learned today:

____
____
____

Today I felt:

My habits:

1. Yes / No
2. Yes / No
3. Yes / No

My mood today:

Daily log _____ / _____ / _____

Today I am grateful for:

1. _______________________________

2. _______________________________

3. _______________________________

My priorities today:

1. _______________________________

2. _______________________________

3. _______________________________

A thing that made me happy:

____

____

____

This is something I learned today:

____

____

Today I felt:

My habits:

1.   Yes / No

2.   Yes / No

3.   Yes / No

My mood today:

Daily log   /   /

Today I am grateful for:
1.
2.
3.

My priorities today:
1.
2.
3.

A thing that made me happy:

This is something I learned today:

Today I felt:

My habits:

1.   Yes / No
2.   Yes / No
3.   Yes / No

My mood today:

Daily log ___/___/___

Today I am grateful for:

1. _______________________________
2. _______________________________
3. _______________________________

My priorities today:

1. _______________________________
2. _______________________________
3. _______________________________

A thing that made me happy:

____
____
____

This is something I learned today:

____
____
____

Today I felt:

👍 👎

My habits:

1. Yes / No
2. Yes / No
3. Yes / No

My mood today:

Daily log ___ / ___ / ___

Today I am grateful for:

1. _______________________________________

2. _______________________________________

3. _______________________________________

My priorities today:

1. _______________________________________

2. _______________________________________

3. _______________________________________

A thing that made me happy:

____

____

____

This is something I learned today:

____

____

____

Today I felt:

My habits:

1.   Yes / No

2.   Yes / No

3.   Yes / No

My mood today:

Daily log   /   /

Today I am grateful for:
1.
2.
3.

My priorities today:
1.
2.
3.

A thing that made me happy:

This is something I learned today:

Today I felt:

My habits:

1. Yes / No
2. Yes / No
3. Yes / No

My mood today:

Daily log ___ / ___ / ___

Today I am grateful for:
1.
2.
3.

My priorities today:
1.
2.
3.

A thing that made me happy:

This is something I learned today:

Today I felt:

My habits:

1. Yes / No
2. Yes / No
3. Yes / No

My mood today:

My weekly summary

Which things turned out the way I expected?

What can I do differently another time?

Mostly I felt:

How was my mood this week?

How well did I keep my habits this week?

My weekly summary - continued

What have I influenced this week?

What did I learn from this?

What have I not been able to influence?

How do I choose to handle it?

- o   Dwell
- o   Let it go
- o   Learn
- o   Moping
- o   Ignore
- o   Moody
- o   Accept
- o   Joke away
- o   Perspective

Other way:

What unfinished tasks do I need to move to next week?

176

Weekly overview week:__________ year: 20___

My intention for this week:

My focus for this week:

My top five priorities this week:
1.
2.
3.
4.
5.

This week I will:
1.
Because:

2.
Because:

3.
Because:

Daily log ___ / ___ / ___

Today I am grateful for:
1.
2.
3.

My priorities today:
1.
2.
3.

A thing that made me happy:

This is something I learned today:

Today I felt:

My habits:

1. Yes / No
2. Yes / No
3. Yes / No

My mood today:

Daily log   /   /

Today I am grateful for:

1.
2.
3.

My priorities today:

1.
2.
3.

A thing that made me happy:

This is something I learned today:

Today I felt:

My habits:

1.   Yes / No
2.   Yes / No
3.   Yes / No

My mood today:

Daily log ____ / ____ / ____

Today I am grateful for:
1. ______________________________
2. ______________________________
3. ______________________________

My priorities today:
1. ______________________________
2. ______________________________
3. ______________________________

A thing that made me happy:
____
____
____

This is something I learned today:
____
____
____

Today I felt:

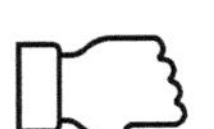

My habits:

1. Yes / No
2. Yes / No
3. Yes / No

My mood today:

Daily log ___ / ___ / ___

Today I am grateful for:
1.
2.
3.

My priorities today:
1.
2.
3.

A thing that made me happy:

This is something I learned today:

Today I felt:

👍 👎

My habits:

1. Yes / No
2. Yes / No
3. Yes / No

My mood today:

Daily log _______ / _____ / _______

Today I am grateful for:
1. ....
2. ....
3. ....

My priorities today:
1. ....
2. ....
3. ....

A thing that made me happy:
....
....
....

This is something I learned today:
....
....
....

Today I felt:

My habits:

1. Yes / No
2. Yes / No
3. Yes / No

My mood today:

Daily log ____ / ____ / ____

Today I am grateful for:

1.
2.
3.

My priorities today:

1.
2.
3.

A thing that made me happy:

This is something I learned today:

Today I felt:

My habits:

1. Yes / No
2. Yes / No
3. Yes / No

My mood today:

Daily log ____/____/____

Today I am grateful for:

1.
2.
3.

My priorities today:

1.
2.
3.

A thing that made me happy:

This is something I learned today:

Today I felt:

My habits:

1.   Yes / No
2.   Yes / No
3.   Yes / No

My mood today:

My weekly summary

Which things turned out the way I expected?

What can I do differently another time?

Mostly I felt: 👍 👎

How was my mood this week?

How well did I keep my habits this week?

My weekly summary - continued

What have I influenced this week?

What did I learn from this?

What have I not been able to influence?

How do I choose to handle it?

o Dwell	o Moping	o Accept
o Let it go	o Ignore	o Joke away
o Learn	o Moody	o Perspective

Other way:

What unfinished tasks do I need to move to next week?

My thoughts after this week

188

Weekly overview week:__________ year: 20__

My intention for this week:

My focus for this week:

My top five priorities this week:
1.
2.
3.
4.
5.

This week I will:
1.
Because:

2.
Because:

3.
Because:

Daily log ____ / ____ / ____

Today I am grateful for:

1.
2.
3.

My priorities today:

1.
2.
3.

A thing that made me happy:

This is something I learned today:

Today I felt:

My habits:

1. Yes / No
2. Yes / No
3. Yes / No

My mood today:

Daily log ___ / ___ / ___

Today I am grateful for:
1. _______________________________________
2. _______________________________________
3. _______________________________________

My priorities today:
1. _______________________________________
2. _______________________________________
3. _______________________________________

A thing that made me happy:
____
____
____

This is something I learned today:
____
____
____

Today I felt:

My habits:

1.   Yes / No
2.   Yes / No
3.   Yes / No

My mood today:

Daily log ___ / ___ / ___

Today I am grateful for:

1. ....
2. ....
3. ....

My priorities today:

1. ....
2. ....
3. ....

A thing that made me happy:

....
....
....

This is something I learned today:

....
....
....

Today I felt:

My habits:

1. Yes / No
2. Yes / No
3. Yes / No

My mood today:

Daily log ____ / ____ / ____

Today I am grateful for:

1.
2.
3.

My priorities today:

1.
2.
3.

A thing that made me happy:

This is something I learned today:

Today I felt:

My habits:

1. Yes / No
2. Yes / No
3. Yes / No

My mood today:

Daily log ____ / ____ / ____

Today I am grateful for:

1. ________________________________
2. ________________________________
3. ________________________________

My priorities today:

1. ________________________________
2. ________________________________
3. ________________________________

A thing that made me happy:

____
____
____

This is something I learned today:

____
____
____

Today I felt:

My habits:

1. Yes / No
2. Yes / No
3. Yes / No

My mood today:

Daily log   /   /

Today I am grateful for:
1.
2.
3.

My priorities today:
1.
2.
3.

A thing that made me happy:

This is something I learned today:

Today I felt:

My habits:

1.   Yes / No
2.   Yes / No
3.   Yes / No

My mood today:

Daily log ____ / ____ / ____

Today I am grateful for:

1.
2.
3.

My priorities today:

1.
2.
3.

A thing that made me happy:

This is something I learned today:

Today I felt:

My habits:

1.   Yes / No
2.   Yes / No
3.   Yes / No

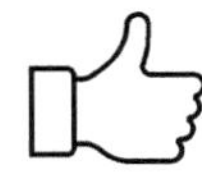 

My mood today:

My weekly summary

Which things turned out the way I expected?

What can I do differently another time?

Mostly I felt: 👍 👎

How was my mood this week?

😃 🙂 😐 🙁 😭 😟 😍 😆 🤩 😎 😌 🥴 😳 😈 😇

How well did I keep my habits this week?

☒ ⭐☆☆ ⭐⭐☆ ⭐⭐⭐

My weekly summary - continued

What have I influenced this week?

What did I learn from this?

What have I not been able to influence?

How do I choose to handle it?

- o Dwell
- o Let it go
- o Learn
- o Moping
- o Ignore
- o Moody
- o Accept
- o Joke away
- o Perspective

Other way:

What unfinished tasks do I need to move to next week?

My thoughts after this week

Weekly overview week:__________ year: 20__

My intention for this week:

My focus for this week:

My top five priorities this week:
1.
2.
3.
4.
5.

This week I will:
1.
Because:

2.
Because:

3.
Because:

Daily log ___ / ___ / ___

Today I am grateful for:

1. ____
2. ____
3. ____

My priorities today:

1. ____
2. ____
3. ____

A thing that made me happy:

____
____
____

This is something I learned today:

____
____
____

Today I felt:

My habits:

1. Yes / No
2. Yes / No
3. Yes / No

My mood today:

Daily log ___ / ___ / ___

Today I am grateful for:

1. _______________________________
2. _______________________________
3. _______________________________

My priorities today:

1. _______________________________
2. _______________________________
3. _______________________________

A thing that made me happy:

____
____
____

This is something I learned today:

____
____
____

Today I felt:

My habits:

1.   Yes / No
2.   Yes / No
3.   Yes / No

My mood today:

Daily log ____ / ____ / ____

Today I am grateful for:

1. ___________________________
2. ___________________________
3. ___________________________

My priorities today:

1. ___________________________
2. ___________________________
3. ___________________________

A thing that made me happy:

____
____
____

This is something I learned today:

____
____
____

Today I felt:

My habits:

1. Yes / No
2. Yes / No
3. Yes / No

My mood today:

Daily log   /   /

Today I am grateful for:

1.
2.
3.

My priorities today:

1.
2.
3.

A thing that made me happy:

This is something I learned today:

Today I felt:

My habits:

1.   Yes / No
2.   Yes / No
3.   Yes / No

My mood today:

Daily log ____ / ____ / ____

Today I am grateful for:

1.
2.
3.

My priorities today:

1.
2.
3.

A thing that made me happy:

This is something I learned today:

Today I felt:

My habits:

1. Yes / No
2. Yes / No
3. Yes / No

My mood today:

Daily log   ____ / ____ / ____

Today I am grateful for:

1. ....
2. ....
3. ....

My priorities today:

1. ....
2. ....
3. ....

A thing that made me happy:

This is something I learned today:

Today I felt:

My habits:

1. Yes / No
2. Yes / No
3. Yes / No

My mood today:

Daily log ___ / ___ / ___

Today I am grateful for:

1.
2.
3.

My priorities today:

1.
2.
3.

A thing that made me happy:

This is something I learned today:

Today I felt:

My habits:

1. Yes / No
2. Yes / No
3. Yes / No

My mood today:

My weekly summary

Which things turned out the way I expected?

What can I do differently another time?

Mostly I felt: 👍 👎

How was my mood this week?

😃 😊 😐 ☹️ 😭 😠 😍 😖 🤩 😎 😌 😳 😮 😈 😇

How well did I keep my habits this week?

☒   ★☆☆   ★★☆   ★★★

My weekly summary - continued

What have I influenced this week?

What did I learn from this?

What have I not been able to influence?

How do I choose to handle it?

o Dwell	o Moping	o Accept
o Let it go	o Ignore	o Joke away
o Learn	o Moody	o Perspective

Other way:

What unfinished tasks do I need to move to next week?

My thoughts after this week

Weekly overview week:_____________ year: 20___

My intention for this week:

My focus for this week:

My top five priorities this week:
1.
2.
3.
4.
5.

This week I will:
1.
Because:

2.
Because:

3.
Because:

Daily log ___ / ___ / ___

Today I am grateful for:

1. ________________
2. ________________
3. ________________

My priorities today:

1. ________________
2. ________________
3. ________________

A thing that made me happy:

____
____
____

This is something I learned today:

____
____
____

Today I felt:

My habits:

1. Yes / No
2. Yes / No
3. Yes / No

My mood today:

Daily log ___ / ___ / ___

Today I am grateful for:

1. _______________________________

2. _______________________________

3. _______________________________

My priorities today:

1. _______________________________

2. _______________________________

3. _______________________________

A thing that made me happy:

____

____

____

This is something I learned today:

____

____

____

Today I felt:

My habits:

1.   Yes / No

2.   Yes / No

3.   Yes / No

My mood today:

Daily log ___ / ___ / ___

Today I am grateful for:
1.
2.
3.

My priorities today:
1.
2.
3.

A thing that made me happy:

This is something I learned today:

Today I felt:

My habits:

1.   Yes / No
2.   Yes / No
3.   Yes / No

My mood today:

Daily log   /   /

Today I am grateful for:

1.
2.
3.

My priorities today:

1.
2.
3.

A thing that made me happy:

This is something I learned today:

Today I felt:

My habits:

1.   Yes / No
2.   Yes / No
3.   Yes / No

My mood today:

Daily log ___ / ___ / ___

Today I am grateful for:

1. ....

2. ....

3. ....

My priorities today:

1. ....

2. ....

3. ....

A thing that made me happy:

....

....

....

This is something I learned today:

....

....

....

Today I felt:

My habits:

1. Yes / No
2. Yes / No
3. Yes / No

My mood today:

Daily log   /   /

Today I am grateful for:
1.
2.
3.

My priorities today:
1.
2.
3.

A thing that made me happy:

This is something I learned today:

Today I felt:

My habits:

1. Yes / No
2. Yes / No
3. Yes / No

My mood today:

Daily log ____ / ____ / ____

Today I am grateful for:
1.
2.
3.

My priorities today:
1.
2.
3.

A thing that made me happy:

This is something I learned today:

Today I felt:

My habits:

1.   Yes / No
2.   Yes / No
3.   Yes / No

My mood today:

My weekly summary

Which things turned out the way I expected?

What can I do differently another time?

Mostly I felt:

How was my mood this week?

How well did I keep my habits this week?

My weekly summary - continued

What have I influenced this week?

What did I learn from this?

What have I not been able to influence?

How do I choose to handle it?

o Dwell	o Moping	o Accept
o Let it go	o Ignore	o Joke away
o Learn	o Moody	o Perspective

Other way:

What unfinished tasks do I need to move to next week?

My thoughts after this week

Weekly overview week:_____________ year: 20___

My intention for this week:

My focus for this week:

My top five priorities this week:
1.
2.
3.
4.
5.

This week I will:
1.
Because:

2.
Because:

3.
Because:

Daily log ____ / ____ / ____

Today I am grateful for:
1.
2.
3.

My priorities today:
1.
2.
3.

A thing that made me happy:

This is something I learned today:

Today I felt:

My habits:

1.   Yes / No
2.   Yes / No
3.   Yes / No

My mood today:

Daily log ____ / ____ / ____

Today I am grateful for:
1.
2.
3.

My priorities today:
1.
2.
3.

A thing that made me happy:

This is something I learned today:

Today I felt:

My habits:

1. Yes / No
2. Yes / No
3. Yes / No

My mood today:

Daily log _____ / _____ / _____

Today I am grateful for:

1. _______________________________________
2. _______________________________________
3. _______________________________________

My priorities today:

1. _______________________________________
2. _______________________________________
3. _______________________________________

A thing that made me happy:

____
____
____

This is something I learned today:

____
____
____

Today I felt:

My habits:

1. Yes / No
2. Yes / No
3. Yes / No

My mood today:

Daily log   /   /

Today I am grateful for:

1.
2.
3.

My priorities today:

1.
2.
3.

A thing that made me happy:

This is something I learned today:

Today I felt:

My habits:

1. Yes / No
2. Yes / No
3. Yes / No

My mood today:

Daily log   /   /

Today I am grateful for:
1.
2.
3.

My priorities today:
1.
2.
3.

A thing that made me happy:

This is something I learned today:

Today I felt:

My habits:

1. Yes / No
2. Yes / No
3. Yes / No

My mood today:

Daily log ____ / ____ / ____

Today I am grateful for:

1. ______________________________________
2. ______________________________________
3. ______________________________________

My priorities today:

1. ______________________________________
2. ______________________________________
3. ______________________________________

A thing that made me happy:

____
____
____

This is something I learned today:

____
____
____

Today I felt:

My habits:

1. Yes / No
2. Yes / No
3. Yes / No

My mood today:

Daily log _____ / _____ / _____

Today I am grateful for:

1. ....
2. ....
3. ....

My priorities today:

1. ....
2. ....
3. ....

A thing that made me happy:

....

....

....

This is something I learned today:

....

....

....

Today I felt:

My habits:

1.   Yes / No
2.   Yes / No
3.   Yes / No

My mood today:

My weekly summary

Which things turned out the way I expected?

What can I do differently another time?

Mostly I felt: 👍 👎

How was my mood this week?

How well did I keep my habits this week?

My weekly summary - continued

What have I influenced this week?

What did I learn from this?

What have I not been able to influence?

How do I choose to handle it?

o Dwell	o Moping	o Accept
o Let it go	o Ignore	o Joke away
o Learn	o Moody	o Perspective

Other way:

What unfinished tasks do I need to move to next week?

Weekly overview week:_____________ year: 20___

My intention for this week:

My focus for this week:

My top five priorities this week:
1.
2.
3.
4.
5.

This week I will:
1.
Because:

2.
Because:

3.
Because:

Daily log ____ / ____ / ______

Today I am grateful for:

1.

2.

3.

My priorities today:

1.

2.

3.

A thing that made me happy:

This is something I learned today:

Today I felt: My habits:

    1.   Yes / No

    2.   Yes / No

    3.   Yes / No

My mood today:

Daily log ____ / ____ / ____

Today I am grateful for:
1. ____
2. ____
3. ____

My priorities today:
1. ____
2. ____
3. ____

A thing that made me happy:
____
____
____

This is something I learned today:
____
____
____

Today I felt:

My habits:

1. Yes / No
2. Yes / No
3. Yes / No

My mood today:

Daily log ____/____/____

Today I am grateful for:
1. ________________________________
2. ________________________________
3. ________________________________

My priorities today:
1. ________________________________
2. ________________________________
3. ________________________________

A thing that made me happy:
____
____
____

This is something I learned today:
____
____
____

Today I felt:

My habits:

1. Yes / No
2. Yes / No
3. Yes / No

My mood today:

Daily log ___ / ___ / ___

Today I am grateful for:
1.
2.
3.

My priorities today:
1.
2.
3.

A thing that made me happy:

This is something I learned today:

Today I felt:

My habits:

1. Yes / No
2. Yes / No
3. Yes / No

My mood today:

Daily log ___ / ___ / ___

Today I am grateful for:
1. ____
2. ____
3. ____

My priorities today:
1. ____
2. ____
3. ____

A thing that made me happy:
____
____
____

This is something I learned today:
____
____

Today I felt:

My habits:

1. Yes / No
2. Yes / No
3. Yes / No

My mood today:

Daily log ____ / ____ / ____

Today I am grateful for:

1. ....
2. ....
3. ....

My priorities today:

1. ....
2. ....
3. ....

A thing that made me happy:

This is something I learned today:

Today I felt:

My habits:

1. Yes / No
2. Yes / No
3. Yes / No

My mood today:

Daily log ___ / ___ / _____

Today I am grateful for:

1. ....
2. ....
3. ....

My priorities today:

1. ....
2. ....
3. ....

A thing that made me happy:

....
....
....

This is something I learned today:

....
....

Today I felt: My habits:

                                       1.   Yes / No
                                       2.   Yes / No
                                       3.   Yes / No

My mood today:

My weekly summary

Which things turned out the way I expected?

What can I do differently another time?

Mostly I felt:

How was my mood this week?

How well did I keep my habits this week?

My weekly summary - continued

What have I influenced this week?

What did I learn from this?

What have I not been able to influence?

How do I choose to handle it?

- o Dwell
- o Let it go
- o Learn

- o Moping
- o Ignore
- o Moody

- o Accept
- o Joke away
- o Perspective

Other way:

What unfinished tasks do I need to move to next week?

My thoughts after this week

248

Weekly overview week:_____________ year: 20___

My intention for this week:

My focus for this week:

My top five priorities this week:
1.
2.
3.
4.
5.

This week I will:
1.
Because:

2.
Because:

3.
Because:

Daily log ___ / ___ / ___

Today I am grateful for:

1.
2.
3.

My priorities today:

1.
2.
3.

A thing that made me happy:

This is something I learned today:

Today I felt:

My habits:

1.   Yes / No
2.   Yes / No
3.   Yes / No

My mood today:

Daily log ___ / ___ / ___

Today I am grateful for:

1. ____
2. ____
3. ____

My priorities today:

1. ____
2. ____
3. ____

A thing that made me happy:

____

____

This is something I learned today:

____

____

Today I felt:

My habits:

1. Yes / No
2. Yes / No
3. Yes / No

My mood today:

Daily log ____ / ____ / ____

Today I am grateful for:

1.
2.
3.

My priorities today:

1.
2.
3.

A thing that made me happy:

This is something I learned today:

Today I felt:

My habits:

1. Yes / No
2. Yes / No
3. Yes / No

My mood today:

Daily log _____ / _____ / _____

Today I am grateful for:

1. _______________________________________

2. _______________________________________

3. _______________________________________

My priorities today:

1. _______________________________________

2. _______________________________________

3. _______________________________________

A thing that made me happy:

____

____

____

This is something I learned today:

____

____

____

Today I felt:

My habits:

1. Yes / No

2. Yes / No

3. Yes / No

My mood today:

Daily log _____ / _____ / _____

Today I am grateful for:

1. ____
2. ____
3. ____

My priorities today:

1. ____
2. ____
3. ____

A thing that made me happy:

____
____
____

This is something I learned today:

____
____
____

Today I felt:

My habits:

1. Yes / No
2. Yes / No
3. Yes / No

My mood today:

Daily log   ___ / ___ / ___

Today I am grateful for:
1.
2.
3.

My priorities today:
1.
2.
3.

A thing that made me happy:

This is something I learned today:

Today I felt:

My habits:

1. Yes / No
2. Yes / No
3. Yes / No

My mood today:

Daily log ____ / ____ / ____

Today I am grateful for:
1.
2.
3.

My priorities today:
1.
2.
3.

A thing that made me happy:

This is something I learned today:

Today I felt:

My habits:

1. Yes / No
2. Yes / No
3. Yes / No

My mood today:

My weekly summary

Which things turned out the way I expected?

What can I do differently another time?

Mostly I felt:

How was my mood this week?

How well did I keep my habits this week?

My weekly summary - continued

What have I influenced this week?

What did I learn from this?

What have I not been able to influence?

How do I choose to handle it?

o Dwell	o Moping	o Accept
o Let it go	o Ignore	o Joke away
o Learn	o Moody	o Perspective

Other way:

What unfinished tasks do I need to move to next week?

My thoughts after this week

Weekly overview week:__________ year: 20__

My intention for this week:

My focus for this week:

My top five priorities this week:
1.
2.
3.
4.
5.

This week I will:
1.
Because:

2.
Because:

3.
Because:

Daily log ___ / ___ / _____

Today I am grateful for:

1. ....

2. ....

3. ....

My priorities today:

1. ....

2. ....

3. ....

A thing that made me happy:

This is something I learned today:

Today I felt:

My habits:

1. Yes / No

2. Yes / No

3. Yes / No

My mood today:

Daily log ____/____/____

Today I am grateful for:

1. _______________________________
2. _______________________________
3. _______________________________

My priorities today:

1. _______________________________
2. _______________________________
3. _______________________________

A thing that made me happy:

____

____

____

This is something I learned today:

____

____

____

Today I felt:

My habits:

1. Yes / No
2. Yes / No
3. Yes / No

My mood today:

Daily log ____ / ____ / ____

Today I am grateful for:

1. ______________________________
2. ______________________________
3. ______________________________

My priorities today:

1. ______________________________
2. ______________________________
3. ______________________________

A thing that made me happy:

____
____
____

This is something I learned today:

____
____
____

Today I felt:

My habits:

1. Yes / No
2. Yes / No
3. Yes / No

My mood today:

Daily log   ___ / ___ / ___

Today I am grateful for:

1. _________________________________
2. _________________________________
3. _________________________________

My priorities today:

1. _________________________________
2. _________________________________
3. _________________________________

A thing that made me happy:

This is something I learned today:

Today I felt:

My habits:

1. Yes / No
2. Yes / No
3. Yes / No

My mood today:

Daily log _____ / _____ / _____

Today I am grateful for:

1. _______________________________________
2. _______________________________________
3. _______________________________________

My priorities today:

1. _______________________________________
2. _______________________________________
3. _______________________________________

A thing that made me happy:

____
____
____

This is something I learned today:

____
____
____

Today I felt:

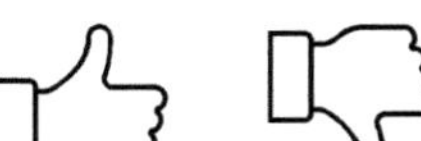

My habits:

1. Yes / No
2. Yes / No
3. Yes / No

My mood today:

Daily log ___/___/___

Today I am grateful for:

1. ____
2. ____
3. ____

My priorities today:

1. ____
2. ____
3. ____

A thing that made me happy:

____
____
____

This is something I learned today:

____
____
____

Today I felt:

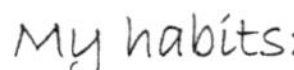

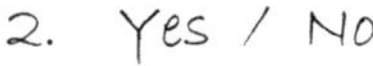

My habits:

1. Yes / No
2. Yes / No
3. Yes / No

My mood today:

Daily log _____ / _____ / _____

Today I am grateful for:

1. ....
2. ....
3. ....

My priorities today:

1. ....
2. ....
3. ....

A thing that made me happy:

....

....

....

This is something I learned today:

....

....

....

Today I felt:

My habits:

1.   Yes / No
2.   Yes / No
3.   Yes / No

My mood today:

My weekly summary

Which things turned out the way I expected?

What can I do differently another time?

Mostly I felt: 👍 👎

How was my mood this week?

How well did I keep my habits this week?

My weekly summary - continued

What have I influenced this week?

What did I learn from this?

What have I not been able to influence?

How do I choose to handle it?

o Dwell	o Moping	o Accept
o Let it go	o Ignore	o Joke away
o Learn	o Moody	o Perspective

Other way:

What unfinished tasks do I need to move to next week?

My thoughts after this week

Weekly overview week:__________ year: 20__

My intention for this week:

My focus for this week:

My top five priorities this week:
1.
2.
3.
4.
5.

This week I will:
1.
Because:

2.
Because:

3.
Because:

Daily log ____ / ____ / ____

Today I am grateful for:

1.
2.
3.

My priorities today:

1.
2.
3.

A thing that made me happy:

This is something I learned today:

Today I felt:

My habits:

1. Yes / No
2. Yes / No
3. Yes / No

My mood today:

Daily log ___ / ___ / ___

Today I am grateful for:

1. ....
2. ....
3. ....

My priorities today:

1. ....
2. ....
3. ....

A thing that made me happy:

....
....
....

This is something I learned today:

....
....
....

Today I felt:

My habits:

1. Yes / No
2. Yes / No
3. Yes / No

My mood today:

Daily log ____ / ____ / ____

Today I am grateful for:
1.
2.
3.

My priorities today:
1.
2.
3.

A thing that made me happy:

This is something I learned today:

Today I felt:

My habits:

1. Yes / No
2. Yes / No
3. Yes / No

My mood today:

Daily log ____ / ____ / ____

Today I am grateful for:

1.

2.

3.

My priorities today:

1.

2.

3.

A thing that made me happy:

This is something I learned today:

Today I felt: My habits:

                                           1.   Yes / No
                                           2.   Yes / No
                                           3.   Yes / No

My mood today:

Daily log ____ / ____ / ____

Today I am grateful for:

1.
2.
3.

My priorities today:

1.
2.
3.

A thing that made me happy:

This is something I learned today:

Today I felt:

My habits:

1. Yes / No
2. Yes / No
3. Yes / No

My mood today:

Daily log ___ / ___ / ___

Today I am grateful for:

1. _______________________________
2. _______________________________
3. _______________________________

My priorities today:

1. _______________________________
2. _______________________________
3. _______________________________

A thing that made me happy:

____

____

This is something I learned today:

____

____

Today I felt:

My habits:

1. Yes / No
2. Yes / No
3. Yes / No

My mood today:

Daily log ___ / ___ / ___

Today I am grateful for:
1.
2.
3.

My priorities today:
1.
2.
3.

A thing that made me happy:

This is something I learned today:

Today I felt:

My habits:

1. Yes / No
2. Yes / No
3. Yes / No

My mood today:

My weekly summary

Which things turned out the way I expected?

What can I do differently another time?

Mostly I felt:

How was my mood this week?

How well did I keep my habits this week?

My weekly summary - continued

What have I influenced this week?

What did I learn from this?

What have I not been able to influence?

How do I choose to handle it?

<table>
<tr><td>o</td><td>Dwell</td><td>o</td><td>Moping</td><td>o</td><td>Accept</td></tr>
<tr><td>o</td><td>Let it go</td><td>o</td><td>Ignore</td><td>o</td><td>Joke away</td></tr>
<tr><td>o</td><td>Learn</td><td>o</td><td>Moody</td><td>o</td><td>Perspective</td></tr>
</table>

Other way:

What unfinished tasks do I need to move to next week?

My thoughts after this week

Weekly overview week:__________ year: 20__

My intention for this week:

My focus for this week:

My top five priorities this week:
1.
2.
3.
4.
5.

This week I will:
1.
Because:

2.
Because:

3.
Because:

Daily log ___/___/___

Today I am grateful for:

1.

2.

3.

My priorities today:

1.

2.

3.

A thing that made me happy:

This is something I learned today:

Today I felt:

My habits:

1. Yes / No
2. Yes / No
3. Yes / No

My mood today:

Daily log _____ / _____ / _____

Today I am grateful for:

1. ____

2. ____

3. ____

My priorities today:

1. ____

2. ____

3. ____

A thing that made me happy:

____

____

____

This is something I learned today:

____

____

____

Today I felt:

My habits:

1. Yes / No
2. Yes / No
3. Yes / No

My mood today:

Daily log ____ / ____ / ____

Today I am grateful for:

1. _______________________________________
2. _______________________________________
3. _______________________________________

My priorities today:

1. _______________________________________
2. _______________________________________
3. _______________________________________

A thing that made me happy:

____

____

This is something I learned today:

____

____

Today I felt:

My habits:

1. 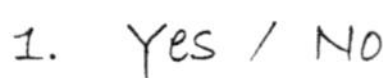 Yes / No
2. 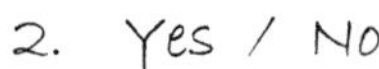 Yes / No
3. 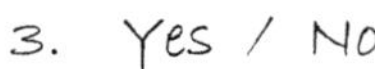 Yes / No

My mood today:

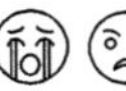

Daily log ____ / ____ / ____

Today I am grateful for:

1. ______________________________
2. ______________________________
3. ______________________________

My priorities today:

1. ______________________________
2. ______________________________
3. ______________________________

A thing that made me happy:

____
____
____

This is something I learned today:

____
____
____

Today I felt:

My habits:

1. Yes / No
2. Yes / No
3. Yes / No

My mood today:

Daily log ____ / ____ / ____

Today I am grateful for:
1.
2.
3.

My priorities today:
1.
2.
3.

A thing that made me happy:

This is something I learned today:

Today I felt:

My habits:

1.   Yes / No
2.   Yes / No
3.   Yes / No

My mood today:

Daily log ____ / ____ / ____

Today I am grateful for:

1. ____
2. ____
3. ____

My priorities today:

1. ____
2. ____
3. ____

A thing that made me happy:

____
____
____

This is something I learned today:

____
____
____

Today I felt:

 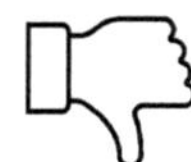

My habits:

1. Yes / No
2. Yes / No
3. Yes / No

My mood today:

Daily log ___ / ___ / ___

Today I am grateful for:
1.
2.
3.

My priorities today:
1.
2.
3.

A thing that made me happy:

This is something I learned today:

Today I felt:

My habits:

1. Yes / No
2. Yes / No
3. Yes / No

My mood today:

My weekly summary

Which things turned out the way I expected?

What can I do differently another time?

Mostly I felt:

How was my mood this week?

How well did I keep my habits this week?

My weekly summary - continued

What have I influenced this week?

What did I learn from this?

What have I not been able to influence?

How do I choose to handle it?

o Dwell	o Moping	o Accept
o Let it go	o Ignore	o Joke away
o Learn	o Moody	o Perspective

Other way:

What unfinished tasks do I need to move to next week?

My thoughts after this week

Weekly overview week:_________ year: 20__

My intention for this week:

My focus for this week:

My top five priorities this week:
1.
2.
3.
4.
5.

This week I will:
1.
Because:

2.
Because:

3.
Because:

Daily log ____ / ____ / ____

Today I am grateful for:

1. ....
2. ....
3. ....

My priorities today:

1. ....
2. ....
3. ....

A thing that made me happy:

....
....
....

This is something I learned today:

....
....
....

Today I felt:

My habits:

1. Yes / No
2. Yes / No
3. Yes / No

My mood today:

Daily log ____ / ____ / ____

Today I am grateful for:
1. ___________________________
2. ___________________________
3. ___________________________

My priorities today:
1. ___________________________
2. ___________________________
3. ___________________________

A thing that made me happy:

____
____
____

This is something I learned today:

____
____
____

Today I felt:

My habits:

1. Yes / No
2. Yes / No
3. Yes / No

My mood today:

Daily log ____ / ____ /

Today I am grateful for:

1. _______________________________
2. _______________________________
3. _______________________________

My priorities today:

1. _______________________________
2. _______________________________
3. _______________________________

A thing that made me happy:

____
____
____

This is something I learned today:

____
____
____

Today I felt:

My habits:

1. Yes / No
2. Yes / No
3. Yes / No

My mood today:

Daily log ___ / ___ / ___

Today I am grateful for:

1. ________________________
2. ________________________
3. ________________________

My priorities today:

1. ________________________
2. ________________________
3. ________________________

A thing that made me happy:

____
____
____

This is something I learned today:

____
____
____

Today I felt:

My habits:

1. Yes / No
2. Yes / No
3. Yes / No

My mood today:

Daily log ____ / ____ / ____

Today I am grateful for:

1. ________________________
2. ________________________
3. ________________________

My priorities today:

1. ________________________
2. ________________________
3. ________________________

A thing that made me happy:

____

____

____

This is something I learned today:

____

____

____

Today I felt:

My habits:

1.   Yes / No
2.   Yes / No
3.   Yes / No

My mood today:

Daily log ____ / ____ / ____

Today I am grateful for:

1. ____
2. ____
3. ____

My priorities today:

1. ____
2. ____
3. ____

A thing that made me happy:

____
____
____

This is something I learned today:

____
____
____

Today I felt:

My habits:

1. Yes / No
2. Yes / No
3. Yes / No

My mood today:

Daily log ____ / ____ / ____

Today I am grateful for:
1.
2.
3.

My priorities today:
1.
2.
3.

A thing that made me happy:

This is something I learned today:

Today I felt:

My habits:

1. Yes / No
2. Yes / No
3. Yes / No

My mood today:

My weekly summary

Which things turned out the way I expected?

What can I do differently another time?

Mostly I felt:

How was my mood this week?

How well did I keep my habits this week?

My weekly summary - continued

What have I influenced this week?

What did I learn from this?

What have I not been able to influence?

How do I choose to handle it?

o Dwell	o Moping	o Accept
o Let it go	o Ignore	o Joke away
o Learn	o Moody	o Perspective

Other way:

What unfinished tasks do I need to move to next week?

My thoughts after this week

Weekly overview week:___________ year: 20___

My intention for this week:

My focus for this week:

My top five priorities this week:
1.
2.
3.
4.
5.

This week I will:
1.
Because:

2.
Because:

3.
Because:

Daily log ___ / ___ / ___

Today I am grateful for:

1.
2.
3.

My priorities today:

1.
2.
3.

A thing that made me happy:

This is something I learned today:

Today I felt:

My habits:

1. Yes / No
2. Yes / No
3. Yes / No

My mood today:

Daily log ____ / ____ / ____

Today I am grateful for:

1. _______________________________
2. _______________________________
3. _______________________________

My priorities today:

1. _______________________________
2. _______________________________
3. _______________________________

A thing that made me happy:

____
____
____

This is something I learned today:

____
____
____

Today I felt:

👍 👎

My habits:

1. Yes / No
2. Yes / No
3. Yes / No

My mood today:

Daily log ____ / ____ / ____

Today I am grateful for:

1. ______________________________
2. ______________________________
3. ______________________________

My priorities today:

1. ______________________________
2. ______________________________
3. ______________________________

A thing that made me happy:

____
____
____

This is something I learned today:

____
____
____

Today I felt:

My habits:

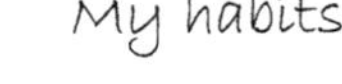

1. Yes / No
2. Yes / No
3. Yes / No

My mood today:

Daily log ___ / ___ / ___

Today I am grateful for:

1. _______________________________________
2. _______________________________________
3. _______________________________________

My priorities today:

1. _______________________________________
2. _______________________________________
3. _______________________________________

A thing that made me happy:

____
____
____

This is something I learned today:

____
____
____

Today I felt:

My habits:

1. Yes / No
2. Yes / No
3. Yes / No

My mood today:

Daily log ____ / ____ / ____

Today I am grateful for:
1.
2.
3.

My priorities today:
1.
2.
3.

A thing that made me happy:

This is something I learned today:

Today I felt:

My habits:

1. Yes / No
2. Yes / No
3. Yes / No

My mood today:

Daily log ____ / ____ / ____

Today I am grateful for:
1. ____
2. ____
3. ____

My priorities today:
1. ____
2. ____
3. ____

A thing that made me happy:
____
____
____

This is something I learned today:
____
____
____

Today I felt:

My habits:

1. Yes / No
2. Yes / No
3. Yes / No

My mood today:

Daily log ____ / ____ / ____

Today I am grateful for:
1.
2.
3.

My priorities today:
1.
2.
3.

A thing that made me happy:

This is something I learned today:

Today I felt:

My habits:

1. Yes / No
2. Yes / No
3. Yes / No

My mood today:

My weekly summary

Which things turned out the way I expected?

What can I do differently another time?

Mostly I felt: 👍 👎

How was my mood this week?

How well did I keep my habits this week?

☒ ★☆☆ ★★☆ ★★★

My weekly summary - continued

What have I influenced this week?

What did I learn from this?

What have I not been able to influence?

How do I choose to handle it?

- o Dwell
- o Let it go
- o Learn

- o Moping
- o Ignore
- o Moody

- o Accept
- o Joke away
- o Perspective

Other way:

What unfinished tasks do I need to move to next week?

My thoughts after this week

Weekly overview week:__________ year: 20__

My intention for this week:

My focus for this week:

My top five priorities this week:
1.
2.
3.
4.
5.

This week I will:
1.
Because:

2.
Because:

3.
Because:

Daily log ____ / ____ / ____

Today I am grateful for:
1. ____
2. ____
3. ____

My priorities today:
1. ____
2. ____
3. ____

A thing that made me happy:
____
____
____

This is something I learned today:
____
____
____

Today I felt:

My habits:

1. Yes / No
2. Yes / No
3. Yes / No

My mood today:

Daily log _____ / _____ / _____

Today I am grateful for:
1. ____
2. ____
3. ____

My priorities today:
1. ____
2. ____
3. ____

A thing that made me happy:

____
____
____

This is something I learned today:

____
____
____

Today I felt:

My habits:

1. Yes / No
2. Yes / No
3. Yes / No

My mood today:

Daily log ____ / ____ / ____

Today I am grateful for:

1. ______________________________
2. ______________________________
3. ______________________________

My priorities today:

1. ______________________________
2. ______________________________
3. ______________________________

A thing that made me happy:

____
____
____

This is something I learned today:

____
____

Today I felt:

My habits:

1. Yes / No
2. Yes / No
3. Yes / No

My mood today:

Daily log ____ / ____ / ____

Today I am grateful for:

1. ____
2. ____
3. ____

My priorities today:

1. ____
2. ____
3. ____

A thing that made me happy:

____

____

____

This is something I learned today:

____

____

____

Today I felt:

My habits:

1. Yes / No
2. Yes / No
3. Yes / No

My mood today:

Daily log ____ / ____ / ____

Today I am grateful for:

1. ....
2. ....
3. ....

My priorities today:

1. ....
2. ....
3. ....

A thing that made me happy:

....
....
....

This is something I learned today:

....
....
....

Today I felt:

My habits:

1. Yes / No
2. Yes / No
3. Yes / No

My mood today:

Daily log _____ / _____ / _____

Today I am grateful for:
1. _______________________________________
2. _______________________________________
3. _______________________________________

My priorities today:
1. _______________________________________
2. _______________________________________
3. _______________________________________

A thing that made me happy:
____
____
____

This is something I learned today:
____
____
____

Today I felt:

My habits:

1.   Yes / No
2.   Yes / No
3.   Yes / No

My mood today:

Daily log ____ / ____ / ____

Today I am grateful for:
1.
2.
3.

My priorities today:
1.
2.
3.

A thing that made me happy:

This is something I learned today:

Today I felt:

My habits:

1.   Yes / No
2.   Yes / No
3.   Yes / No

My mood today:

My weekly summary

Which things turned out the way I expected?

What can I do differently another time?

Mostly I felt: 👍 👎

How was my mood this week?

How well did I keep my habits this week?

My weekly summary - continued

What have I influenced this week?

What did I learn from this?

What have I not been able to influence?

How do I choose to handle it?

- o Dwell
- o Let it go
- o Learn
- o Moping
- o Ignore
- o Moody
- o Accept
- o Joke away
- o Perspective

Other way:

What unfinished tasks do I need to move to next week?

My thoughts after this week

Well done!

Now I have filled this journal with 27 weeks of my life. I am pleased with myself for doing this and proud to have completed it!

I have learned a lot about myself during these 27 weeks and will carry this experience and knowledge with me for the rest of my life, one day at a time, one moment at a time.

I am grateful towards myself for investing so much time and commitment in myself.